# Lake Como
*Travel Guide*

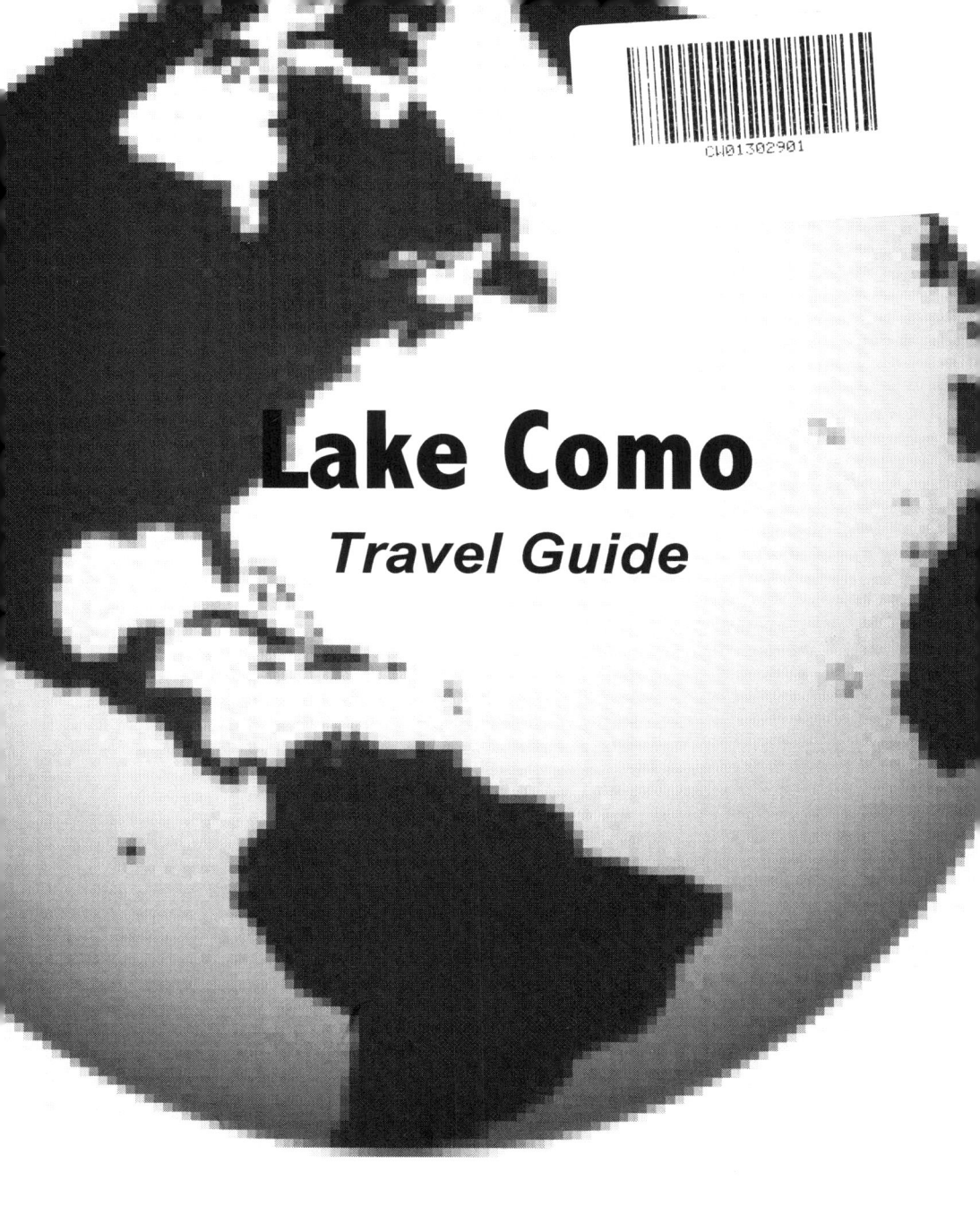

*Quick Trips Series*

No part of this publication may be reproduced, stored in a retrieval system, or transmitted, in any form or by any means without the prior written permission of the publisher, nor be otherwise circulated in any form of binding or cover other than that in which it is published and without similar condition being imposed on the subsequent purchaser. If there are any errors or omissions in copyright acknowledgements the publisher will be pleased to insert the appropriate acknowledgement in any subsequent printing of this publication. Although we have taken all reasonable care in researching this book we make no warranty about the accuracy or completeness of its content and disclaim all liability arising from its use.

Copyright © 2016, Astute Press
All Rights Reserved.

# Table of Contents

## LAKE COMO — 6
- CUSTOMS & CULTURE .................................................. 8
- GEOGRAPHY ............................................................... 11
- WEATHER & BEST TIME TO VISIT ............................. 14

## SIGHTS & ACTIVITIES: WHAT TO SEE & DO — 15
- COMO ........................................................................... 15
  - Outdoor Activities ..................................................... 17
  - Funicular Railway ..................................................... 17
  - Como Cathedral ........................................................ 18
  - Teatro Sociale .......................................................... 19
  - Volta Temple ............................................................ 20
- BELLAGIO .................................................................... 21
  - Villa Serbelloni ......................................................... 22
  - Villa Melzi ................................................................ 23
  - Churches in town ..................................................... 24
- MENAGGIO .................................................................. 25
- VARENNA .................................................................... 26
  - Castello Di Vezio ...................................................... 27
  - Villa Monastero ........................................................ 28
- TREMEZZO .................................................................. 29
  - Villa Carlotta ............................................................ 30
- COMACINA ISLAND ................................................... 31
- LAKE MAGGIORE ....................................................... 33
- MADESIMO SKI RESORT ........................................... 35

# RECOMMENDATIONS FOR A BUDGET TRAVELLER 37

## 🌐 ACCOMMODATION ..................................................37
### Albergo Milano Hotel..................................................37
### Hotel Bellavista ........................................................38
### NH Pontevecchio ......................................................39
### Hotel Plinius ............................................................40
### Best Western Hotel Continental ...............................41

## 🌐 PLACES TO EAT ....................................................42
### Barchetta .................................................................42
### Antica Darsena.........................................................42
### La Vista...................................................................43
### Albergo Valtellina ....................................................44
### Crott del Meo ..........................................................45

## 🌐 SHOPPING ............................................................45
### Azalea .....................................................................45
### Adhoc......................................................................46
### Max Mara.................................................................47
### Decio......................................................................47
### Street Markets - Como .............................................48

# KNOW BEFORE YOU GO 49

## 🌐 ENTRY REQUIREMENTS .........................................49
## 🌐 HEALTH INSURANCE..............................................49
## 🌐 TRAVELLING WITH PETS.......................................50
## 🌐 AIRPORTS..............................................................50
## 🌐 AIRLINES ..............................................................52
## 🌐 CURRENCY ............................................................53
## 🌐 BANKING & ATMS .................................................53
## 🌐 CREDIT CARDS .....................................................53
## 🌐 TOURIST TAXES....................................................54

- 🌐 RECLAIMING VAT .................................................................54
- 🌐 TIPPING POLICY ..................................................................55
- 🌐 MOBILE PHONES .................................................................55
- 🌐 DIALLING CODE ..................................................................56
- 🌐 EMERGENCY NUMBERS .......................................................56
- 🌐 PUBLIC HOLIDAYS ...............................................................57
- 🌐 TIME ZONE .........................................................................57
- 🌐 DAYLIGHT SAVINGS TIME ....................................................58
- 🌐 SCHOOL HOLIDAYS .............................................................58
- 🌐 TRADING HOURS .................................................................58
- 🌐 DRIVING LAWS ...................................................................59
- 🌐 DRINKING LAWS .................................................................60
- 🌐 SMOKING LAWS ..................................................................60
- 🌐 ELECTRICITY ......................................................................61
- 🌐 TOURIST INFORMATION (TI) ...............................................61
- 🌐 FOOD & DRINK ...................................................................62
- 🌐 WEBSITES ..........................................................................63

# **LAKE COMO TRAVEL GUIDE**

# Lake Como

Located in the Lombardy region in northern Italy, Lake Como is one of the most picturesque tourist destinations in Italy. The beauty of the lake and its surrounding areas has made it a favorite vacation spot for the rich and famous. The beauty of Lake Como has featured in many novels, stories, movies, and music videos. The stunning Alps, grand lakeside villas, medieval churches and the

# LAKE COMO TRAVEL GUIDE

serenity of nature make it a tourist magnet attracting visitors year round.

Lake Como is shaped like an inverted alphabet 'Y'. Spanning 146 sq km, and running 400 ft deep, it is the 3rd largest lake in Italy and one of the deepest in Europe. The region surrounding the lake in the southern parts are quite flat but make way to the Alpine foothills in the north.

Along the shore are many beautiful small towns and villages. Towns like Como, Bellagio, Varenna, and Menaggio are not only picture perfect, they also have a very relaxed and laid back atmosphere. Such tranquility and beauty have attracted many celebrities to Lake Como over the years. Lake Como has featured as a private vacation home for celebrities like Sylvester Stallone, Madonna, and Versace. One of the most famous people

# LAKE COMO TRAVEL GUIDE

resident here in recent years is George Clooney. His lakeside villa in the town of Laglio has drawn much public and media attention especially after his marriage there in 2014. In fact, the local government is reputed to slap a fine on any boat coming within 100 yards of it! But do not be surprised to bump on to Clooney in a quiet bar as he often heads in to town without much fanfare.

It is not only Clooney who has been hooked by the beauty of Lake Como. The aristocratic villas bear testimony to the popularity of the region to the rich and the famous for centuries. In fact its natural beauty has been appreciated from as old as the Roman times! Today, Lake Como not only is a haven for nature lovers, the architecture and the myriad cultural activities keeps visitors of all ages and interest equally involved.

# 🌐 Customs & Culture

There are a number of festivals and events in the culture calendar of Lake Como. Operas, theaters, street markets, traditional festivals, and a variety of celebrations keep everyone entertained.

One of the newer but very popular festivals is the Lake Como Festival. Organized since 2006, this bilingual – Italian and English – classical music festival attracts many domestic and international artists. With the backdrop of the Alpine mountains and the beautiful villas, it is an experience of one of its kind. The Schignano Carnival is an annual traditional carnival where many medieval events are reenacted. The Baredello Festival in Como and the Pesa Vegia in Bellano are also medieval costume carnivals that liven up the towns every year. Other popular traditional festivals include the Premana Rivive

# LAKE COMO TRAVEL GUIDE

and the feast of Sagre delle Sagre. Every year the picturesque lakeshore towns are decked up with many Christmas markets where one can buy many traditional crafts and food items.

Theater lovers would be spoilt for choice in the Lake Como region. Not only are there a number of theaters, many of these were built over a century ago and are regarded as attractions themselves for their architectural beauty. Leading the pack is the historic 19th century Teatro Sociale. Other theaters in the lake region include the Teatro Della Societa and the Teatro Sala Polifunzionale in Lecco, the Teatro dei Burattini de Como, and the Griante in Municipio. Families with kids can head to the Fata Morgana Theater which has been rolling out productions for children.

# **LAKE COMO TRAVEL GUIDE**

In spite of its relaxed atmosphere, there is a very vibrant night scene in Lake Como. There are numerous clubs, discos, and bars where one have a drink or dance until dawn! Popular clubs include the Passion Club with its large dance floor and theme nights. The Orsa Maggiore Disco plays Latin music and is also equipped with a restaurant and a lido! Club 29 and Lido di Lenno also draw large crowds, especially on weekends.

There are many options for food lovers in Como. Other than the festivals and traditional events where one can try traditional food and wine, there are many restaurants and cafes in almost every town. Fish items dominate many restaurant menus but if one is strictly looking for a traditional food item then it has be polenta – a cornmeal porridge served with meat or cheese. Risotto – Persian

# LAKE COMO TRAVEL GUIDE

fish made with onion, butter, and white wine is also worth trying.

## 🌐 Geography

Lake Como is located in northern Italy very close to the Switzerland border. In fact, the Swiss border is less than 5 km from the town of Como. Milan is the closest major city to Como; at a distance of about 37 km. Other major Italian cities like Genoa, Verona, and Turin are all within a distance of 150 km from the Lake Como region.

The nearest major airport to Lake Como is the Milano-Malpensa Airport - http://www.milanomalpensa-airport.com/en, IATA: MXP. This airport in Milan is about 56 km from Como and has international connections to many cities including Moscow, Shanghai, Dubai, New York City, Berlin, Barcelona, Miami, Toronto, Istanbul, and

# **LAKE COMO TRAVEL GUIDE**

London, to name just a few. From the airport the best way to get to Como is to take the Malpensa Express towards Milan, and then change to a train to Como from the Saronno Station. The whole journey (less than €10) should take less than 90 minutes. There are also a number of private coaches and taxis at the airport but those would be comparatively more expensive. Visitors can also arrive at the Linate Airport in Milan - http://www.milanolinate-airport.com/en, IATA: LIN. Although it has lesser flights than Malpensa, the airport is closer to the city of Milan than the Malpensa. Another even smaller airport serving the region is the Bergamo Orio al Serio Airport - http://www.sacbo.it/Airpor/portalProcess.jsp, IATA: BGY which is about 45 km from the city of Milan. From this airport one can take the shuttle to the Bergamo station which has hourly train connections with Lecco.

# **LAKE COMO TRAVEL GUIDE**

Trenitalia and LeNORD run many train connections from Como and Lecco to various Italian cities in the Lombardy lines (Line R). Other than to cities like Milan and Bergamo, one can also get international connections to cities like Amsterdam, Frankfurt, Dusseldorf, and Basel. Travelling by train to other cities in the Lombardy region is inexpensive and comfortable. A one-way ticket from Milan costs less than €4.

Travelling by road to Lake Como can be a very enjoyable experience because of the scenic beauty. Most of the connections are through Milan. The E35 motorway connects Milan to Lake Como and then goes further past in to Switzerland. There are many bus services to Lake Como. Other than the airport-express services, there is the popular Eurolines and a few private tour operators like

# **LAKE COMO TRAVEL GUIDE**

Travel 55 and Travelsphere. Road travel is also popular from Bergamo and Lugano (Switzerland).

Once in the Lake Como region, one can use various means of transport to move around. While the town centers are easily covered by foot, one can use the bus or the train to move from one town to another. The western shore is better connected by bus whereas the eastern shore has more train connections. There are many boat and hydrofoil services for those who want to take the water route. Driving is an option, but the narrow winding roads can be a challenge, especially during the tourist season. Motorcycles are a better option. Fitness enthusiasts can also hire bicycles as there are many rental stores all along Lake Como.

# 🌐 Weather & Best Time to Visit

The Lake Como region has a Mediterranean-like humid subtropical climate. Summer months (May to Sep) have an average high of about 28 degrees Celsius and an average low of about 19 degrees. The winter months (Nov to March) are cold and chilly.

Average temperatures during these months rise to around 7 or 8 degree Celsius with lowest falling just below freezing. Summer months are prone to quick and heavy showers – the wettest being May. Although Lake Como attracts tourists all the year round, the most pleasant weather is just around pre-summer and post-summer seasons.

# LAKE COMO TRAVEL GUIDE

## Sights & Activities: What to See & Do

## 🌐 Como

The town of Como is located on the southern tip on the western branch of Lake Como. The city is known for its beautiful medieval architecture and picturesque lakefront, but mostly for its location – on one end Como has excellent connections with Milan and Bergamo, on the other, it is a gateway to the rest of the Como region.

# **LAKE COMO TRAVEL GUIDE**

Although Como is the 3rd most visited place in Lombardy – after Milan and Bergamo - it has often been used just as a stopover destination before visiting the more picturesque and touristy destinations on Lake Como.

However, Como has enough attractions worthy of making it more than a stopover town. Churches, museums, medieval architecture, along with an abundance of outdoor activities and a vibrant nightlife make Como an enjoyable destination for visitors of all interest.

Como is well connected by train and bus from the airports in Milan and Bergamo. Regular train connections are also available with many other countries in Europe. The E35 motorway connects the town with Milan at one direction and the very popular tourist resort of Lugano (Switzerland) on the opposite direction. Within Como one can use the Autolinee bus service or the taxi to move around although, most of the town can be covered by foot. Bicycle rentals are available at http://www.bikeonly.it/. There are over half a dozen parking garages in town for those who are driving in.

## Outdoor Activities

One of the first things to do in Como is to take a walk on the waterfront. Boat rides are available for those who want to visit the neighboring lakeshore towns. One can also bike to the nearby border of Switzerland by riding across the hill at Como. Horseback riding and hiking are also options in the outskirts of Como. The beaches in Como offer a relaxed atmosphere. There are also a number of lidos for those who are looking for some fun and amusements.

# LAKE COMO TRAVEL GUIDE

# Funicular Railway

The funicular ride is a great way to enjoy the natural beauty of Como as well as have a glance of rural Como. Established in 1894 and modernized in 1911, the funicular proudly maintains all safety features of the modern day in spite of its age. The funicular ride connects Como with Brunate. During the ride one can have stunning views of the lake and the surrounding mountains. At the top, other than the panoramic views, one can enjoy the Pissarottino Fountain. One can also climb further up to the Volta Lighthouse at the peak. On the way down one can simply walk by the tracks or take a number of different routes. There is also a shuttle service to take people downhill. The funicular operates from 6 am until 10:30 am every day except Saturdays when it operates until midnight.

**LAKE COMO TRAVEL GUIDE**

# Como Cathedral

Built in 1740, the Como Cathedral is often regarded as the last cathedral in Italy built in a Gothic style. It replaced a Romanesque cathedral on the same site, construction of which had started in the late 14th century. This dominating structure can be identified by its 75 m high dome. It stretches 87 m in length and is 56 m at its widest. The floor plan of the cathedral resembles a Latin Cross. Inside there is a central nave and 2 aisles with a Renaissance transept. The interior is beautifully decorated with a 16th century choir. The tapestries from the 17th century came from Antwerp, Florence, and Ferrara. The 'modern' touch is provided by colorful stained glass windows that were added in the 19th century.

# Teatro Sociale

The Teatro Sociale was built in 1813 to replace the outdated 18th century theater in town. The new theater was built with membership subscriptions. It replaced the ruins of Torre Rotondo, a medieval castle. Construction started with the neo-classical façade that was planned well in advance. However, by 1854, the theater had to be expanded. Yearlong expansions added 38 new boxes to take the total up to 98. It was again expanded in 1910 when another house was added. The present structure is from the remodeling of 1984. It now has a seating capacity of 900 separated into 5 tiers.

The interior of the theater is adorned with a cello-shaped auditorium, red-velvet seats, sculpted walls, and a number of priceless paintings. The theater hosts many performances throughout the year, ranging from children's plays to operas. Even if one is not planning to watch a performance, it is worth the time to visit the Teatro Sociale just to admire the building.

## Volta Temple

The Volta Temple – Tempio Voltiano to the locals – is a museum housed in a beautiful neoclassical building and dedicated to the scientist and inventor Alessandro Volta. Volta, who lived his last years in Como is credited to having invented the electrical battery.

The museum and the portrait of Volta used to feature in the 10000 lira banknote of Italy before the currency was replaced by the Euro. The Volta Temple is one of the most visited museums in Lake Como. It displays many

## LAKE COMO TRAVEL GUIDE

scientific instruments and personal belongings of the scientist.

Attractions in Como are not limited to the ones listed above. Other attractions in town include the Civic Archeological Museum and the History Museum. There is also a war memorial at the waterfront. A walk in the walled old town will also take one past many historic buildings that have stood the passage of time. 2 walks are specially recommended – the 'Romantic Promenade Walk' along the western shore of the lake and the Night Walk from Torre Civica to the Piazza Cavour via the Cathedral Square.

# 🌑 Bellagio

The picture postcard town of Bellagio is situated at the junction of the 3 branches of Lake Como. This beautiful lakeshore town along with its incredibly stunning natural surroundings makes it a must-visit place when in Lake Como. Its strategic location at the peninsula coupled with its beauty earned it the nickname – Pearl of Lake Como.

Bellagio is well connected with Como by train and bus. Within the city one can take a guided tour or simply walk around aimlessly and admire the hamlets and luxurious villas.

## Villa Serbelloni

One of the most popular villas in Bellagio is the Villa Serbelloni on via Roma. The original villa was built in 1485 replacing a country house which, in turn, had replaced a castle on the same site. The villa went through major renovations and expansions in the 17th century and was given the grand look that we see today. It has been

## **LAKE COMO TRAVEL GUIDE**

owned by a number of aristocratic families over the centuries, including Ella Walker, the owner of the popular Canadian Club Whiskey; since 1959 it is under the Rockefeller Foundation. The villa is not open to the public but the surrounding garden is.

The Serbelloni garden which includes the wooded hill behind the town can only be visited through a guided tour. The tour is not only informative; one can also enjoy panoramic views of Bellagio that cannot be seen from any other place. However, one cannot go close to the garden by the villa as it is reserved for the guests of the foundation. The guided tours are available for a minimum of 6 and a maximum of 30 people. There are two 90-minute tours daily at 11:30 am and 3:30 pm. It costs €9 per person with discounts for children and seniors.

# Villa Melzi

Built in 1810, the Villa Melzi is a neoclassical gem with a Japanese Garden, a monument to Dante, and Azaleas steps. The Etruscan cinerary on the left of the building entrance dates back to the 3rd century BC. The outside of the villa has a number of Egyptian and Roman sculptural engravings.

The interior, which is not open to the public, has beautiful wooden furnishings, paintings, sculptures, and frescoes.

The beautifully landscaped garden surrounding the villa has Japanese maples, rhododendrons, and American redwoods. Do not miss the statute of the Egyptian goddess Pacht that Napoleon had gifted to one of the former owners of the villa. The English styled garden overlooks the lake bringing a tremendous sense of tranquility. The neatly laid out bushes and shrubs are done in complete harmony with the villa. The garden is open to the public in the summer months from 9:30 am to 6:30 pm.

Other villas in Bellagio include the Villa del Balbianello and the Villa Trotti.

## Churches in town

Two churches worth visiting in Bellagio are the Church of Madonna del Rosario and the San Giovanni Church. The former is a church built in a Romanesque style of architecture that has a number of priceless pieces of art adorning its interior. The latter is decorated with a number of beautiful sculptures. A short walk takes one to the ruins of a $10^{th}$ century monastery nestled in the hilltop caves.

# LAKE COMO TRAVEL GUIDE

Bellagio has a number of restaurants, cafes, and nightclubs - all aimed at visiting tourists as the population of the town is very low. One of the highlights in town is the open air opera. With the backdrop of the lake and the alpine peaks, the operas are almost a surreal experience.

## 🌐 Menaggio

Located about halfway along the western shore of Lake Como is the town of Menaggio. Although the town does not have too many attractions, it is an excellent place to enjoy a number of outdoor activities. Menaggio is well connected by bus from not only Como and Bergamo, but also from the Swiss holiday town of Lugano. This once strategic town was fortified with walls and a castle. This hill side can be clearly separated into two distinct sections. The old town on the side of the hill has more

# **LAKE COMO TRAVEL GUIDE**

medieval architecture and the section near the foot of the hill has a more 'modern' 19th century look. The old town presents narrow alleys, stone buildings, and steep cobbled stairways whereas the newer part of town has luxurious villas, tree-lined promenade, and many al fresco restaurants and cafes.

Once in town, one of the first things to do would be to take a walk along the lake promenade to enjoy the serenity and beauty of Menaggio. A short climb up the hill and one is transported back by a few centuries.

Amongst the religious monuments in town, one can see the Parish church of St Stephen. This Romanesque styled church has a richly decorated chapel that is visually very appealing. The town also has the Baroque styled church of St Charles and the Saviour's Fountain.

# LAKE COMO TRAVEL GUIDE

One of the highlights of Menaggio is the historic Menaggio and Cadenabbia Golf Club. Founded in 1903, the club not only offers a beautiful green course but also a spectacular backdrop with the lake and the Alpine peaks. The length of this 18 hole course is 5476 m. Visitors can play in this course with a fee (weekdays €55; weekends €70). Clubs and buggies are also available on hire. The town also has a sports center and a lido for those looking for a swim or a tan.

## 🌍 Varenna

Located on the eastern shore of Lake Como, Varenna completes the golden triangle of Lake Como, along with Belaggio and Menaggio. The town is probably the most visited on the eastern shore. The golden triangle is so

## LAKE COMO TRAVEL GUIDE

popular with the tourists that it has its own ferry route and service.

The shaded lakeside promenade of Varenna is similar to that of Menaggio; on the other hand, the narrow cobbled pathways leading to the old town up the hill are similar to that of Bellagio.

The town of Varenna, however, is quieter and less touristy than the other two. Varenna also attracts more Italian visitors due to its direct rail connection with Milan. One of the delights is to try the locally made gelato (ice-cream) that is sold by a number of stalls on the lakeside promenade.

# Castello Di Vezio

This is the most visited tourist attraction of Varenna. This 13th century castle is perched on a hilltop and has excellent views of the lake and the town, especially from the olive garden and the top of the viewing tower. The biggest draw of the castle is the close encounter with the birds of prey that are trained and maintained there. With a ticket one can meet the falconer and have a chance to see the birds 'perform' at close range. If lucky, one may even get the chance to hold one of the birds of prey. The falconer is present from 10 am to 6 pm everyday and trains the birds in front of the visitors. Special shows are held almost every day at 2:30 pm. However, the display and the castle are closed in bad weather and in the winter months. There is an entry fee of €4 with discounts for children and seniors.

# LAKE COMO TRAVEL GUIDE

# Villa Monastero

Villa Monsatero is one of the few villas that has been accredited as a museum and is open to the public. Like most other villas, it is on the lakefront and is surrounded by a beautifully laid out garden.

The garden stretches for nearly 2 km and has different sections like the citrus collection, a formal terrace, a grand landing platform, and a promenade adorned with sculptures. There is a narrow pathway separating the garden from the lake which has a number of benches where one can sit and enjoy the spectacular views. The villa which is now rented out for conferences and meetings is worth visiting to see the grandeur of the decorations and the furnishings. It is open daily in the summer months (Mar to Nov) from 9:30 am to 7 pm.

There is an entry fee of €8 with discounts for children and seniors.

## 🌐 Tremezzo

The small town of Tremezzo is located on the western shore of Lake Como about 20 km from Como and on the opposite shore of Bellagio. It is connected by bus and ferry services from both Como and Bellagio. For centuries, Tremezzo has been known for its mild climate, beautiful gardens, and luxurious villas.

There is a small public park that leads out to the lake where one can go for a swim in the clear azure water of Lake Como. A relaxed stroll of the town will take one to the 18th century parish church of San Lorenzo.

### LAKE COMO TRAVEL GUIDE

The town has a number of villas like the La Carlia, Amila, and the Meier which are privately owned. The luxurious Grand Hotel Tremezzo is also housed in a villa. But the one villa that is open to the public and is a major tourist attraction is the Villa Carlotta. Tremezzo also has a lot of lush greenery, primarily because of its location where it is protected from strong cold winds. Historically, it has been popular for its olive gardens and the production of oil.

# Villa Carlotta

Sprawling a massive 17 acres, the Villa Carlotta was built in 1690 for the marquis of Milan – Giorgio Clerici. It is named after Charlotte, the Duchess of Saxe-Meiningen, who received the villa as a wedding gift from her mother – Princess Marianna of Prussia. The villa faces the peninsula of Bellagio and is decorated with an Italian garden that is adorned with sculptures and fountains. In

# LAKE COMO TRAVEL GUIDE

fact, the fascinating works of art in the garden and the surrounding park made the villa one of the most famous in the Lake Como region. Rhododendrons, azaleas, camellias, ferns, and even bamboo trees compliment the beauty of the villa garden. The garden also has a museum of agricultural tools. The 2 floors of the house museum have a variety of items in display. While the first floor has many works of art from the 18th and 19th centuries, the second floor displays furniture and household items from the days of Charlotte. The villa area also includes a book store, a café, and a couple of picnic spots. The villa and the garden are open in the summer months (Mar to Oct) from 10 am to 6 pm and have an entry fee of €9.

# LAKE COMO TRAVEL GUIDE

# 🌍 Comacina Island

In the first glance, Comacina Island looks like a green teardrop in the Lake Como. This small lush green island may look uninhabited and deserted but has been the witness to many historical events. The whole island was used as a fortress in the middle ages. Controlled by the Byzantine garrison, the island was in the side of Milan and fought against Como in the '10 year war'. The island was donated to the Italian government by the King of Belgium in 1919.

Attractions on the island include a number of archeological sites with remains from the Roman era. There are also the ruins of 7 Byzantine churches. The island was a favorite of many Italian and Belgian artists and one of the features is the artist's homes. The most popular are the 3 homes built in the late 1930s by Pietro

# LAKE COMO TRAVEL GUIDE

Lingeri – simply named as A, B, and C. These simple stone houses have two floors with a kitchen, bedroom, toilet, and a studio. These houses were built as vacation homes for the visiting artists. The island, spreading hardly 6 hectares, is a nature lover's delight. It is wrapped in lush Mediterranean greenery giving it a warm and soothing atmosphere. There is also a hospital complex and an Antiquarium Museum on the island.

## 🌐 Lake Maggiore

Located about 5 km west of Lake Como is the beautiful tourist resort of Lake Maggiore.

With a length of 63 km and 10 km at its widest, it is the 2$^{nd}$ largest lake in Italy. About a fifth of the northern part of the lake is in Switzerland.

## **LAKE COMO TRAVEL GUIDE**

The lake, formed from a glacier, is surrounded by hills in the southern parts, and the taller Alpine mountains along the northern shores. The mild climate, many picturesque lakeshore towns, and a host of outdoor activities make Lake Maggiore a very popular tourist destination.

Lake Maggiore is located 20 km north of the Malpensa Airport. The western shore is well connected by rail with Milan and Geneva. The lakeshore towns like Stresa, Arona, Verbania, and Baveno have regular bus connections.

Attractions of Lake Maggiore include the cable car ride to the Mottarone Mountain peak from Stresa. Other than its panoramic viewpoints, the mountain is popular for hiking in the summer months and for skiing in the winter months. Stresa is also the stop to take the ferry to the picturesque

## **LAKE COMO TRAVEL GUIDE**

Borromeo Archipelago with its 3 islands – Bella, Madre, and Pescatori. The Santa Ana Gorge on the Cannabino River is a favorite for kayaking and white water rafting. Outdoor enthusiasts will also enjoy mountain biking and hiking in Mercurago near Arona. For the nature lovers there is the Villa Pallavicino Park near Stresa. The park has a botanical garden and a zoo and is open in the summer months only. The picturesque Villa Taranto Botanical Gardens is located in Verbania. Lovers of history and archeology will enjoy the 12th century Santa Caterina del Sasso Church, the Cannero Castle, the Angera Castle, and the Arona Fortress.

It is recommended to carry Swiss Francs along with Euros if travelling along the Lake as many places in the Swiss border do not accept Euros. The whole of Lake Maggiore is a tourist attraction, so, if planning to travel from Lake

Como, one should have at least a couple of days to have a feel of the area.

## 🌐 Madesimo Ski Resort

The Madesimo Ski Resort is located about 70 km north of Lake Como and about 110 km from Milan. The resort is near the Swiss border. While the area is popular for hiking in the summer months, it is a popular ski resort in the winter months.

Madesimo is best reached by car. The Via Spluga or SS36 runs from the Lake Como region to Madesimo. One need not drive all the way to the skiing area. There is a free (only on weekdays) parking zone in Campodolcino from where there is a funicular connection to Madesimo. However, it is recommended that good snow tires are used if taking a car to Madesimo in winter. For those who prefer public transport can opt for the bus, train, or taxi share.

Madesimo is more popular with the local Italians and is very busy on the weekends, so it is preferable if one can visit the place on weekdays. It is part of the skiing area of Valchiavenna.

With just over 50 km of trails, it is one of the smaller resorts in northern Italy but offers a host of activities. Golf, biking, camping, indoor football, canoeing, rock climbing, and swimming are popular in Madesimo. The adventurous can also try snow-kite surfing. For those who want to strictly stick to skiing, there are a number of rental stores to get the skiing accessories. Amateurs can also opt for a professional guide.

# LAKE COMO TRAVEL GUIDE

## Recommendations for a Budget Traveller

### 🌍 Accommodation

### Albergo Milano Hotel

Via XX Settembre 35., Varenna

Tel: 39 0341 830 298

http://www.varenna.net/ENG/Servizi.html

## **LAKE COMO TRAVEL GUIDE**

Located in the historic center of Varenna.

The Albergo Milano has been welcoming guests since the early 20$^{th}$ century. The hotel is ideal for those who are looking for a romantic getaway and even for those who are looking for a quiet relaxed vacation. It has retained many of its original furnishings and décor thus giving the guest a feeling of the yesteryears. The hotel has a beautiful terrace and an al fresco restaurant. It has free parking and free Wi-Fi.

Rooms have TV, safe, minibar, and fan. Room rates start from €130 and include breakfast.

# LAKE COMO TRAVEL GUIDE

# Hotel Bellavista

Via IV Novembre 21

Menaggio

Tel: 39 0344 32136

http://www.hotel-bellavista.org/

This 3 star hotel is located on the lake front of Menaggio. The pier to catch ferries to Como and Bellagio is hardly 150 m away. Facilities include free Wi-Fi and a free outdoor pool. There is a bar and a restaurant. Guests receive a discount at the nearby golf course.

All rooms are ensuite and some are with a verandah facing the lake. Room rates start from €70 and include breakfast.

**LAKE COMO TRAVEL GUIDE**

# NH Pontevecchio

Via A Visconti 84

Lecco

Tel: 39 0341 238000

http://www.nh-hotels.com/nh/en/hotels/italy/lecco---lake-como/nh-pontevecchio.html

Located about a 5 minute walk from the historic center of Lecco, the Pontevecchio is a 4 star hotel near the waterfront area. Facilities include 24 hr reception, elevators, free Wi-Fi, free parking, and doctor on call. There is an onsite restaurant and bar.

The ensuite rooms are non-smoking and come with a TV, air-conditioning, minibar, radio, telephone, laundry

# LAKE COMO TRAVEL GUIDE

service, and safe. Room rates start from €90 and include breakfast.

## Hotel Plinius

Via Garibaldi 33

Como

Tel: 39 031 273 067

http://www.hotelplinius.com/

This 3 star hotel is located between the Como town center and the lakefront. The station is 300 m away. Public transport is available nearby. Attractions in the vicinity include the Como Cathedral, major shopping streets, and a number of restaurants.

# LAKE COMO TRAVEL GUIDE

The newly renovated rooms are modern-styled and equipped with free Wi-Fi and satellite TV. Room rates start from €70 and include breakfast.

## Best Western Hotel Continental

Viale Innocenzo XI 15

Como

Tel: 39 031 260 485

http://www.hotelcontinentalcomo.it/en/home-page.aspx

Located about a 5 minute walk from the Como historic town center, the Best Western is a 3 star hotel with all the usual modern amenities. The hotel has car park (surcharge), free Wi-Fi, lift, bar, and a restaurant. Outdoor activities like horseriding, tennis, and fishing are available near the hotel.

The ensuite non-smoking rooms have minibar, TV, AC, safe, and hairdryer. Room rates start from €85 and include breakfast.

## 🌐 Places to Eat

## Barchetta

Piazza Cavour 1, Como

Tel: 39 031 3221

http://www.hotelbarchetta.it/en/hotel-como-with-restaurant

The Barchetta is part of the Barchetta Excelsior Hotel and is located right on the lakefront. The restaurant has a simple yet elegant décor. Cuisine served is primarily Italian. Starters, rice, and pasta are priced within €15. Non-vegetarian dishes like grilled fish in vegetables, veal shank in herb, and beef fillet in red wine are priced around €25. One can also try a variety of local wine (around €6).

## Antica Darsena

Lungo Lario Trieste 16, Como

Tel: 39 031 23391

http://www.palacehotel.it/en/hotel-restaurant-como

The Antica Darsena is located inside the Palace Hotel. With crystal chandeliers, half moon windows, and a spectacular view of the lake, the Antica Darsena is ideal for a romantic or quiet meal.

It serves local and Mediterranean cuisine. Both vegetarian and non-vegetarian starters are priced around €15. Rice and pasta are also priced the same. Entrees include items like prawns in olive (€22), baked lamb with vegetables

(€28), and risotto in melted butter (€25). Desserts include mousse, salads, tiramisu, and fruits.

## La Vista

Via XX Settembre 35

Varenna

Tel: 39 0341 830 298

http://www.varenna.net/ENG/Ristorante-LaVista.php

This al fresco restaurant overlooks the lake and has spectacular views during sunset and the nighttime. It is part of the Albergo Milano Hotel. The menu, which changes every year, comprises of Mediterranean and Italian dishes. Guests can choose from set menus – 3-course (€38), or 4-course (€45). Dishes include bell peppers in fresh cheese (€14), fish fillet with pink pepper

(€19), and wild boar pasta in cheese (€15). It also serves a variety of wine and champagne.

## Albergo Valtellina

Via Bellinzona 265, Como

Tel: 39 31 540 750

http://www.albergovaltellina.com/eng/ristorante.php

Part of the Valtellina Hotel, the Albergo Valtellina Restaurant is a small and cozy restaurant serving Italian cuisine. This is also an ideal place to try some traditional local dishes. The restaurant serves a tourist menu (€11 excluding drinks) where one can try a variety of local dishes. Dishes on the a la carte include dried beef, pasta with porcini mushrooms, polenta, and a variety of wine.

# Crott del Meo

Via Campora 2

Perledo

Tel: 39 333 225 1298

http://www.crottdelmeo.it/en/kitchen.html

This cozy restaurant serves traditional dishes typical to the lake region. It has a stone cellar for storing wine, cheese, and salami – the 3 specialties of the restaurant. Homemade specialties also include a unique variety of jams – onion jam, pepper jam, and coffee jam! Cakes and ice-cream are also made in-house. It offers a 6-course meal (€28) where guests can select the dishes.

# 🌐 Shopping

## Azalea

Salita Serbelloni 31

Bellagio

Tel: 39 031 951 333

http://www.azaleabellagio.com/

One of the most popular products from the Lake Como region is silk. Not only are the silk products of a very good quality, they are also much cheaper than in most major cities like Milan. The Azalea is on the busy Serbelloni Street and sells a variety of pure silk products – ties, scarves, bags, and foulards. It also sells shirts and leather items. The Azalea has a branch at Serbelloni 41.

## LAKE COMO TRAVEL GUIDE

# Adhoc

Lungo Lario Manzoni 42-44

Bellagio

Tel: 39 031 950 073

http://www.adhocbellagio.it/index_eng.html

The Adhoc is the authorized dealer of a number of popular Italian brands like Bridge, Emilio Pucci, Gherardini, and Orciani. This is the ideal place for visitors looking for branded Italian leather and silk products. Items on sale include bags, foulards, scarves, leather accessories, hats, and small gift items like key chains.

# Max Mara

Via Vittorio Emanule 87

Como

# LAKE COMO TRAVEL GUIDE

Tel: 39 031 262 321

Located in Como, this is one of the most popular design houses of Italy. The knowledgeable and helpful staff makes shopping at Max Mara a truly enjoyable experience. From the latest trends to the popular classics, Max Mara has a complete collection of various types of clothes and accessories, and that too, at a very reasonable price.

## Decio

Via Lusardi 22

Menaggio

Tel: 39 0344 31195

Located in the town center of Menaggio, this homeware boutique is for those who are looking to take home a piece of Italy. Targeting primarily the interior décor market, the store sells items like glassware, candles, soft furnishings, and tableware. There is also a large collection of bed linen. Visitors can also buy gift items from Decio.

## Street Markets - Como

Shopping is incomplete in the Lake Como region without a visit to the street markets. From fresh produce to bargain products, the street markets have it all. These markets are usually located in the popular squares and the town hall area. The popular markets include the Haberdashery Market (Viale Varese), Food Market (via Mentana), and Albate Market (via Facioloa). The Saturday-only Crafts and Antiques Market is at Piazza San Fedele.

## Know Before You Go

# 🌐 Entry Requirements

By virtue of the Schengen agreement, travellers from other countries in the European Union do not need a visa when visiting Italy. Additionally Swiss travellers are also exempt. Visitors from certain other countries such as the USA, Canada, Japan, Israel, Australia and New Zealand do not need visas if their stay in Italy does not exceed 90 days. When entering Italy you will be required to make a declaration of presence, either at the airport, or at a police station within eight days of arrival. This applies to visitors from other Schengen countries, as well as those visiting from non-Schengen countries.

# 🌐 Health Insurance

Citizens of other EU countries are covered for emergency health care in Italy. UK residents, as well as visitors from Switzerland are covered by the European Health Insurance Card (EHIC), which can be applied for free of charge. Visitors from non-Schengen countries will need to show proof of private health insurance that is valid for the duration of their stay in

Italy (that offers at least €37,500 coverage), as part of their visa application. No special vaccinations are required.

## 🌐 Travelling with Pets

Italy participates in the Pet Travel Scheme (PETS) which allows UK residents to travel with their pets without requiring quarantine upon re-entry. Certain conditions will need to be met. The animal will have to be microchipped and up to date on rabies vaccinations. In the case of dogs, a vaccination against canine distemper is also required by the Italian authorities. When travelling from the USA, your pet will need to be microchipped or marked with an identifying tattoo and up to date on rabies vaccinations. An EU Annex IV Veterinary Certificate for Italy will need to be issued by an accredited veterinarian. On arrival in Italy, you can apply for an EU pet passport to ease your travel in other EU countries.

## 🌐 Airports

**Fiumicino – Leonardo da Vinci International Airport** (FCO) is one of the busiest airports in Europe and the main international airport of Italy. It is located about 35km southwest of the historical quarter of Rome. Terminal 5 is used for trans-Atlantic and international flights, while Terminals 1, 2 and 3 serve mainly for domestic flights and medium haul flights to

## LAKE COMO TRAVEL GUIDE

other European destinations. Before Leonardo da Vinci replaced it, the **Ciampino–G. B. Pastine International Airport** (CIA) was the main international airport servicing Rome and Italy. It is one of the oldest airports in the country still in use. Although it declined in importance, budget airlines such as Ryanair boosted its air traffic in recent years. The airport is used by Wizz Air, V Bird, Helvetic, Transavia Airlines, Sterling, Ryanair, Thomsonfly, EasyJet, Air Berlin, Hapag-Lloyd Express and Carpatair.

**Milan Malpensa Airport** (MXP) is the largest of the three airports serving the city of Milan. Located about 40km northwest of Milan's city center, it connects travellers to the regions of Lombardy, Piedmont and Liguria. **Milan Linate Airport** (LIN) is Milan's second international airport. **Venice Marco Polo Airport** (VCE) provides access to the charms of Venice. **Olbia Costa Smeralda Airport** (OLB) is located near Olbia, Sardinia. Main regional airports are **Guglielmo Marconi Airport** (BLQ), an international airport servicing the region of Bologna, **Capodichino Airport** at Naples (NAP), **Pisa International Airport** (PSA), formerly Galileo Galilei Airport, the main airport serving Tuscany, **Sandro Pertini Airport** near Turin (TRN), **Cristoforo Colombo** in Genoa (GOA), **Punta Raisi Airport** in Palermo (PMO), **Vincenzo Bellini Airport** in Catania (CTA) and **Palese Airport** in Bari (BRI).

# LAKE COMO TRAVEL GUIDE

## 🌐 Airlines

Alitalia is the flag carrier and national airline of Italy. It has a subsidiary, Alitalia CityLiner, which operates short-haul regional flights. Air Dolomiti is a regional Italian based subsidiary of of the Lufthansa Group. Meridiana is a privately owned airline based at Olbia in Sardinia.

Fiumicino - Leonardo da Vinci International Airport serves as the main hub for Alitalia, which has secondary hubs at Milan Linate and Milan Malpensa Airport. Alitalia CityLiner uses Fiumicino – Leonardo da Vinci International Airport as main hub and has secondary hubs at Milan-Linate, Naples and Trieste. Fiumicino – Leonardo da Vinci International Airport is also one of two primary hubs used by the budget Spanish airline Vueling. Milan Malpensa Airport is one of the largest bases for the British budget airline EasyJet. Venice Airport serves as an Italian base for the Spanish budget airline, Volotea, which provides connections mainly to other destinations in Europe. Olbia Costa Smeralda Airport (OLB), located near Olbia, Sardinia is the primary base of Meridiana, a private Italian Airline in partnership with Air Italia and Fly Egypt.

## 🌐 Currency

Italy's currency is the Euro. It is issued in notes in denominations of €500, €200, €100, €50, €20, €10 and €5.

Coins are issued in denominations of €2, €1, 50c, 20c, 10c, 5c, 2c and 1c.

## 🌎 Banking & ATMs

Using ATMs or Bancomats, as they are known in Italy, to withdraw money is simple if your ATM card is compatible with the MasterCard/Cirrus or Visa/Plus networks. There is a €250 limit on daily withdrawals. Italian machines are configured for 4-digit PIN numbers, although some machines will be able to handle longer PIN numbers. Bear in mind some Bancomats can run out of cash over weekends and that the more remote villages may not have adequate banking facilities so plan ahead.

## 🌎 Credit Cards

Credit cards are valid tender in most Italian businesses. While Visa and MasterCard are accepted universally, most tourist oriented businesses also accept American Express and Diners Club. Credit cards issued in Europe are smart cards that that are fitted with a microchip and require a PIN for each transaction. This means that a few ticket machines, self-service vendors and other businesses may not be configured to accept the older magnetic strip credit cards. Do remember to advise your bank or credit card company of your travel plans before leaving.

# 🌐 Tourist Taxes

Tourist tax varies from city to city, as each municipality sets its own rate. The money is collected by your accommodation and depends on the standard of accommodation. A five star establishment will levy a higher amount than a four star or three star establishment. You can expect to pay somewhere between €1 and €7 per night, with popular destinations like Rome, Venice, Milan and Florence charging a higher overall rate. In some regions, the rate is also adjusted seasonally. Children are usually exempt until at least the age of 10 and sometimes up to the age of 18. In certain areas, disabled persons and their companions also qualify for discounted rates. Tourist tax is payable directly to the hotel or guesthouse before the end of your stay.

# 🌐 Reclaiming VAT

If you are not from the European Union, you can claim back VAT (Value Added Tax) paid on your purchases in Italy. The VAT rate in Italy is 21 percent and this can be claimed back on your purchases if certain conditions are met. The merchant needs to be partnered with a VAT refund program. This will be indicated if the shop displays a "Tax Free" sign. The shop assistant will fill out a form for reclaiming VAT. When you submit this at the airport, you will receive your refund.

## LAKE COMO TRAVEL GUIDE

# 🌐 Tipping Policy

If your bill includes the phrase "coperto e servizio", that means that a service charge or tip is already included. Most waiting staff in Italy are salaried workers, but if the service is excellent, a few euros extra would be appreciated.

# 🌐 Mobile Phones

Most EU countries, including Italy use the GSM mobile service. This means that most UK phones and some US and Canadian phones and mobile devices will work in Italy. While you could check with your service provider about coverage before you leave, using your own service in roaming mode will involve additional costs. The alternative is to purchase an Italian SIM card to use during your stay in Italy.

Italy has four mobile networks. They are TIM, Wind, Vodafone and Tre (3) and they all provide pre-paid services. TIM offers two tourist options, both priced at €20 (+ €10 for the SIM card) with a choice of two packages - 2Gb data, plus 200 minutes call time or internet access only with a data allowance of 5Gb. Vodafone, Italy's second largest network offers a Vodafone Holiday package including SIM card for €30. They also offer the cheapest roaming rates. Wind offers an Italian Tourist pass for €20 which includes 100 minutes call time and 2Gb data and can be extended with a restart option for an extra €10.

To purchase a local SIM card, you will need to show your passport or some other form of identification and provide your residential details in Italy. By law, SIM registration is required prior to activation. Most Italian SIM cards expire after a 90 day period of inactivity. When dialling internationally, remember to use the (+) sign and the code of the country you are connecting to.

# Dialling Code

The international dialling code for Italy is +39.

# Emergency Numbers

Police: 113
Fire: 115
Ambulance: 118
MasterCard: 800 789 525
Visa: 800 819 014

# Public Holidays

1 January: New Year's Day (Capodanno)
6 January: Day of the Epiphany (Epifania)
March-April: Easter Monday (Lunedì dell'Angelo or Pasquetta)
25 April: Liberation Day (Festa della Liberazione)

# LAKE COMO TRAVEL GUIDE

1 May: International Worker's Day (Festa del Lavoro / Festa dei Lavoratori)

2 June: Republic Day (Festa della Repubblica)

15 August: Assumption Day (Ferragosto / Assunta)

1 November: All Saints Day (Tutti i santi / Ognissanti)

8 December: Immaculate Conception (Immacolata Concezione / Immacolata)

25 December: Christmas Day (Natale)

26 December: St Stephen's Day (Santo Stefano)

A number of Saints days are observed regionally throughout the year.

## 🌐 Time Zone

Italy falls in the Central European Time Zone. This can be calculated as Greenwich Mean Time/Coordinated Universal Time (GMT/UTC) +2; Eastern Standard Time (North America) -6; Pacific Standard Time (North America) -9.

## 🌐 Daylight Savings Time

Clocks are set forward one hour on 29 March and set back one hour on 25 October for Daylight Savings Time.

# LAKE COMO TRAVEL GUIDE

## 🌐 School Holidays

The academic year begins in mid September and ends in mid June. The summer holiday is from mid June to mid September, although the exact times may vary according to region. There are short breaks around Christmas and New Year and also during Easter. Some regions such as Venice and Trentino have an additional break during February for the carnival season.

## 🌐 Trading Hours

Trading hours for the majority of shops are from 9am to 12.30pm and then again from 3.30pm to 7.30pm, although in some areas, the second shift may be from 4pm to 8pm instead. The period between 1pm and 4pm is known in Italy as the *riposo*. Large department shops and malls tend to be open from 9am to 9pm, from Monday to Saturday. Post offices are open from 8.30am to 1.30pm from Monday to Saturday. Most shops and many restaurants are closed on Sundays. Banking hours are from 8.30am to 1.30pm and then again from 3pm to 4pm, Monday to Friday. Most restaurants are open from noon till 2.30pm and then again from 7pm till 11pm or midnight, depending on the establishment. Nightclubs open around 10pm, but only liven up after midnight. Closing times vary, but will generally be between 2am and 4am. Museum hours vary,

## LAKE COMO TRAVEL GUIDE

although major sights tend to be open continuously and often up to 7.30pm. Many museums are closed on Mondays.

# 🌐 Driving Laws

The Italians drive on the right hand side of the road. A driver's licence from any of the European Union member countries is valid in Italy. Visitors from non-EU countries will require an International Driving Permit that must remain current throughout the duration of their stay in Italy.

The speed limit on Italy's autostrade is 130km per hour and 110km per hour on main extra-urban roads, but this is reduced by 20km to 110km and 90km respectively in rainy weather. On secondary extra-urban roads, the speed limit is 90km per hour; on urban highways, it is 70km per hour and on urban roads, the speed limit is 50km per hour. You are not allowed to drive in the ZTL or Limited Traffic Zone (or *zona traffico limitato* in Italian) unless you have a special permit.

Visitors to Italy are allowed to drive their own non-Italian vehicles in the country for a period of up to six months. After this, they will be required to obtain Italian registration with Italian licence plates. Italy has very strict laws against driving under the influence of alcohol. The blood alcohol limit is 0.05 and drivers caught above the limit face penalties such as fines of up to €6000, confiscation of their vehicles, suspension of their licenses and imprisonment of up to 6 months. Breathalyzer tests are routine at accident scenes.

## 🌐 Drinking Laws

The legal drinking age in Italy is 16. While drinking in public spaces is allowed, public drunkenness is not tolerated. Alcohol is sold in bars, wine shops, liquor stores and grocery shops.

## 🌐 Smoking Laws

In 2005, Italy implemented a policy banning smoking from public places such as bars, restaurants, nightclubs and working places, limiting it to specially designated smoking rooms. Further legislation banning smoking from parks, beaches and stadiums is being explored.

## 🌐 Electricity

Electricity: 220 volts

Frequency: 50 Hz

Italian electricity sockets are compatible with the Type L plugs, a plug that features three round pins or prongs, arranged in a straight line. An alternate is the two-pronged Type C Euro adaptor. If travelling from the USA, you will need a power converter or transformer to convert the voltage from 220 to 110, to avoid damage to your appliances. The latest models of many laptops, camcorders, mobile phones and digital cameras are dual-voltage with a built in converter.

## 🌐 Tourist Information (TI)

There are tourist information (TI) desks at each of the terminals of the Leonardo da Vinci International Airport, as well as interactive Information kiosks with the latest touch-screen technology. In Rome, the tourist office can be found at 5 Via Parigi, near the Termini Station and it is identified as APT, which stands for Azienda provinciale del Turismo. Free maps and brochures of current events are available from tourist kiosks.

Several of the more tourist-oriented regions of Italy offer tourist cards that include admission to most of the city's attractions. While these cards are not free, some offer great value for money. A variety of tourism apps are also available online.

## 🌐 Food & Drink

Pasta is a central element of many typically Italian dishes, but there are regional varieties and different types of pasta are matched to different sauces. Well known pasta dishes such as lasagne and bolognaise originated in Bologna. Stuffed pasta is popular in the northern part of Italy, while the abundance of

## **LAKE COMO TRAVEL GUIDE**

seafood and olives influences southern Italian cuisine. As far as pizza goes, the Italians differentiate between the thicker Neapolitan pizza and the thin crust Roman pizza, as well as white pizza, also known as focaccia and tomato based pizza. Other standards include minestrone soup, risotto, polenta and a variety of cheeses, hams, sausages and salamis. If you are on a budget, consider snacking on stuzzichini with a few drinks during happy hour which is often between 7 and 9pm. The fare can include salami, cheeses, cured meat, mini pizzas, bread, vegetables, pastries or pate. In Italy, Parmesan refers only to cheese originating from the area surrounding Parma. Favorites desserts include tiramisu or Italian gelato.

Italians enjoy relaxing to aperitifs before they settle down to a meal and their favorites are Campari, Aperol or Negroni, the famous Italian cocktail. Wine is enjoyed with dinner. Italy is particularly famous for its red wines. The best known wine regions are Piedmont, which produces robust and dry reds, Tuscany and Alto Adige, where Alpine soil adds a distinctive acidity. After the meal, they settle down to a glass of limoncello, the country's most popular liqueur, or grappa, which is distilled from grape seeds and stems, as digestive. Other options in this class include a nut liqueur, nocino, strawberry based Fragolino Veneto or herbal digestives like gineprino, laurino or mirto. Italians are also fond of coffee. Espresso is drunk through throughout the day, but cappuccino is considered

## LAKE COMO TRAVEL GUIDE

a morning drink. The most popular beers in Italy are Peroni and Moretti.

# 🌐 Websites

http://vistoperitalia.esteri.it/home/en

This is the website of the Consulate General of Italy. Here you can look up whether you will need a visa and also process your application online.

http://www.italia.it/en/home.html

The official website of Italian tourism

http://www.italia.it/en/useful-info/mobile-apps.html

Select the region of your choice to download a useful mobile app to your phone.

http://www.italylogue.com/tourism

http://italiantourism.com/index.html

http://www.reidsitaly.com/

http://wikitravel.org/en/Italy

https://www.summerinitaly.com/

http://www.accessibleitalianholiday.com/

Planning Italian vacations around the needs of disabled tourists.

Printed in Great Britain
by Amazon

Printed in Great Britain
by Amazon